Mosaic Hearts

Poems on Being a Queer and Interracial Family in the South

Anne Kinsey

TEHOM
CENTER

Tehom Center Publishing is a 501(c)3 nonprofit publishing feminist and queer authors, with a commitment to elevate BIPOC writers. Its face and voice is Rev. Dr. Angela Yarber.

Paperback ISBN: 978-1-966655-08-4

Ebook ISBN: 978-1-966655-07-7

CONTENTS

PART II: COMPLEXITY

PART III: JOY

To Allen, Will, River, and Becca, the loves of my life.

"Beloved community is formed not by the eradication of difference but by its affirmation, by each of us claiming the identities and cultural legacies that shape who we are and how we live in the world."

— BELL HOOKS, "KILLING RAGE: ENDING RACISM"

INTRODUCTION

Think of this book as a vibrant mosaic table, inviting you to pull up a chair, enjoy your favorite beverage, and converse with a treasured friend. As you listen and share, notice the blue iridescent tile one moment, then the green and gray tile the next. Let your eyes gradually drift from one colorful tile to the next, then zoom out to see the entire work, the love embedded in it, and the unique constellation of tiles that are not replicated in any other table, even those created to have a similar design.

Understanding my family's mosaic hearts begins with my sharing that in our rural North Carolina neighborhood, there are no other families like ours. On our morning walks or visits to the small-town grocery store, we never see another family that is both queer and interracial. It hasn't even happened once. While traveling out of state or spending the day in the city to go to the queer community center, we occasionally connect with others like us, and the internet helps us find community. However, it does not happen in the area where we live.

Out of 19 houses on our street, there is not one Black person aside from my spouse and three children, and it has been this way for the 20 years we have lived here. There certainly aren't any queer families, let alone interracial families holding all of these identities, plus living with disability, financial marginalization, neurodivergence, and more. This morning, my kid counted 11 Trump signs on our morning walk, just a few weeks before the November 2024 election, and voter registration records show that there is one other registered Democrat, a few unaffiliated voters, and the rest of the neighborhood identifies as Republican.

It might seem like we are alone in our experiences here, but we are not. The U.S. Census Bureau reports that in 2016, there were 11 million interracial marriages in the United States, making up 10.2 percent of all couples.[1] In Cabarrus County, where we live, interracial couples increased by four or more percentage points between 2012-2016.[2] In addition, a 2017 Gallup poll indicated that 10.7 million adults identified as queer in the United States.[3] I assume that at least some of these folx are in interracial relationships and live in rural areas, even if there is no data to show us exactly how many.

Do we sometimes feel lonely or isolated living where we live? For sure, and I am certain many other queer and interracial families feel similarly. Even in cities, we don't consistently bump into other families that look like ours. Since we experience varying degrees of marginalization and traumatization in the areas where we live and have no community centers or spaces to connect with one another, our experiences often go unvoiced. Our trauma frequently sits unprocessed, especially considering how difficult it can be to find accessible mental health providers with lived experiences that equip them to walk alongside us on our healing journeys.

My hope is that the poems in this book give voice to intersectional experiences in ways that help others feel less alone. This book is divided into three sections that explore Pain, Complexity, and Joy so that you can choose what to read based on your current needs and capacity. Sometimes, pain feels isolating such

---

1. Race, Ethnicity and Marriage in the United States (census.gov) , Accessed 9/25/2024.
2. Race, Ethnicity and Marriage in the United States (census.gov) , Accessed 9/25/2024.
3. LGBTQ Family Fact Sheet (census.gov), Accessed 9/25/2024

that reading about someone who has gone through something similar brings relief. Other times, trauma is so raw and overwhelming that a nugget of hope that acknowledges complexity keeps us going. Similarly, joy occasionally makes our hearts want to dance, while other times it feels cruel in the face of what life throws our way. What brings one person joy feels painful for another. Even the most painful experiences frequently involve elements of goodness, and everything is complex, not just the things labeled that way.

Given the above, I hope you will read this book and use it in whatever ways are most helpful for you. Feel free to jump around or read the book from cover to cover. The section introductions and occasional reflective pauses are designed to open space for you to explore your own feelings and experiences. If you find that you need additional support as you read and process, I encourage you to reach out to trusted, affirming professionals, connect with your local queer community center, reach out to friends, seek out coaching, join online support groups, or even connect with crisis lines intended to serve people sharing your identities and needs.

To the allies who are reading this book: thank you for stopping by, listening, digesting experiences that differ from your own, and considering how you might put your own privilege and experiences to work in making the world a kinder place for us all. The events and emotions shared here belong to me and to my family, but queer and interracial families are not a monolith, so I encourage you to read, listen to, and engage with as many different resources as you can to invite a chorus of voices into your awareness.

Finally, some of the poems in this work are more explicitly centered on our intersectional identities than others. However, it is impossible to separate our life experiences of marginalization from our other life experiences. Every part of us exists in a symbiotic relationship that makes up the whole of who we are. We cannot be a queer and interracial family in one scenario, but not in another. In this way, when you read a poem that does not seem explicitly intersectional, consider how the perspective or experience conveyed might differ if written by someone with different life experiences than mine or my family's. Each of us moves through the world experiencing everyday pleasures and pains in unique ways that reflect our personal history, collective history, privileges, marginalization, and more. As Audre Lorde said, "There is no such thing as a single-issue struggle because we do not lead single-issue lives."

~ *Anne Kinsey*, September 2024

PART 1: PAIN

"We are not only fighting for our lives, but we are also fighting for our joy, our pleasure, our right to be seen and heard."

— PATRISSE CULLORS, *WHEN THEY CALL YOU A TERRORIST: A BLACK LIVES MATTER MEMOIR*

THOUGHTS ON PAIN

TONI MORRISON FAMOUSLY SAID, "IF THERE'S A BOOK you want to read, but it hasn't been written yet, then you must write it."[1] Those are the dynamics that birthed this collection, especially the poems exploring the painful life experiences shared in this section. Isolation often magnifies our anger, sadness, and fear, making it feel deeper, wider, and more overwhelming. Connection with those who have been there often brings relief, validation, and a sense of belonging or purpose. As part of a queer and interracial family, I have often searched for the right book to comfort me in moments of need, only to come up empty-handed. In those moments, writing poetry has been my comfort, helping me process emotions and inadvertently creating the very support I sought.

As you digest the words on the following pages, I hope they meet you in your times of need. Books are always available to connect with, day or night, much like having someone's phone number and an open invitation to call at any hour. When friends and family are asleep, written words offer companionship, validation, care, empathy, and compassion. Some people compare home

---

1. *Morrison, Toni. Conversations with Toni Morrison. Edited by Danille K. Taylor-Guthrie, University Press of Mississippi, 1994, p. 124.*

libraries or reading lists to medicine cabinets, each book offering something different that helps in just the right way when needed.

May these poems remind you that you are not alone, your feelings are valid, and your experiences matter. You matter. This section on Pain touches on themes of racism, homophobia, transphobia, fatphobia, and other forms of marginalization and trauma. Be mindful of when it might be helpful and validating to read these poems, and when you might be better served by exploring the other sections that address Complexity and Joy.

To the allies reading this, thank you for opening your hearts and engaging with the intense dynamics explored in these poems. I hope you feel encouraged to seek social change, making the necessity for such expressions less pressing. Also, while our lived experiences may differ, our human experiences of emotion are likely very similar, connecting us through your reading here.

North Carolina Republicans

nominate lunacy,
perversion hidden
behind hate,
married to it,
gerrymandering
graves, defying goodness
with dysfunctional democracy
where desired diversity
loses seats to
book bans,
abortion bans,
love bans,
humanity bans,
red carving precision,
increasingly extreme
Christian nationalism,
dizzyingly,
deathly nefarious:
Bishop, Morrow,
Robinson,
you can't
make it up.
Watch it
backfire.

N-Word at the Park

Pet goats, bunnies,
hawks, snakes,
paddle boats, lake,
picnic, walk,
stroller, toddler,
then hear it:
n-word baby,
n-word lover,
cackling laughter,
taunting,
and white evil,
energetic poison.
We're glad to be home
alive.

Amethyst Crystal

lavender translucence,
smoothed edges,
lightly striped
with white,
crown chakra,
calming peace,
connectedness

prompting wonder.
Where did you
come from?
Did someone
exploit life,
kill life,
traffick life,
for you to land

with stones
in black trays
for free
at a spiritual shop?
Your story calls
my soul to act,
life brimming
for justice,
as I stand.

Reflective Pause: Ethical Awareness

"Amethyst Crystal" explores the ethical and human rights questions that arose when I was given a free crystal at a local spiritual shop and the storekeeper could not answer my questions about its origins. As you read, I invite you to consider the people who might have been impacted by that crystal, leaning into empathy and the need for awareness surrounding issues of human trafficking. Then, consider how our daily choices impact the world around us in profound ways.

In my work as the founding executive director of a nonprofit that offers healing services to people who have experienced human trafficking, I have listened to countless stories from survivors who wished people had recognized the signs of their exploitation while it was ongoing. Many yearn for the average person to become more aware of what human trafficking is and how it functions, while being more mindful of the industries and practices they support with their everyday dollars. Imagine how both personal and systemic changes might make human trafficking and labor exploitation less common.

One way we can make progress is by intentionally growing in empathy in ways that change how we see the world, moving us in the direction of increased compassion and intentional action. We can seek new information from more marginalized voices, connecting deeply with others so that we are more aware of our impact on them, as well as their joys and struggles. Extending kindness through careful consideration of our news consumption, spending habits, and daily interactions can help us contribute to a more just and loving world, affirming both our own worth and the worth of every living being.

Reflective Writing

Think of a time when you felt alone in your struggles, but someone noticed and was there for you. What did that feel like and how did it impact your life? Next, think of a time you noticed a need in the world or in an individual and decided to intentionally help. How did that feel and what impact did it have on you and others?

Compose a poem that captures these moments, comparing what it feels like to receive, to give, to be seen, and to see, focusing on the emotions and ripple effects of empathy. If you feel so led, share this poem with someone close to you or somewhere it will make a difference in the world, perhaps on social media.

Dear Miserable Me

Let yourself be loved
openheartedly,
freely, spaciously,
even when,
especially when,
flat misery
threatens to blow
out your light.

Performative

After George Floyd,
you inbox me
to ask if
we are okay,
what it is like
to be from there
with a family
like mine
and see this.

After the racist
Facebook group
comment from
an old white lady,
where crickets
force me to say
something,
to be the one
yet again,
you inbox me
to say you agree.

On my pride post,
smiling children
and dozens of
rainbows,
you say,
"Happy Pride!"
tell me I am
a good mother,
then inbox me
about your niece
who is nonbinary.

(Learn the term nibling)

At the conference,
when microaggressions
echo from the podium,
every inch of my
skin crawling,
rage boiling, hurt brewing,
sadness, exhaustion
overtaking me,
you are silent,
but later tell me
it is awful
and you are sorry
that happened.

At Food Lion,
you smile at my
political t-shirt,
and say hello
from your white,
cishet, moneyed life,
where your concern
for keeping the peace
with bigots
ensures families
like mine
will never have it.

(With friends like you, who needs enemies?)

Fourth of July

Happy colonizer
empire expansion day,
when I intently debate
Smash the Patriarchy
or The First Pride Was a Riot
t-shirts expressing boiling rage
urgently erupting in peace,
knowing it is not enough.
Sunshiny walks, sweat dripping,
bbq grills, charcoal, and family,
without plans for attending
red, white, and blue celebrations
with monotone mobs who fantasize
about project 2025'ing us away,
watching fireworks explode
to celebrate their freedom.

So Angry

I could stop the world,
slam the door, get out,
and walk the Universe
in search of safe havens,

opening boarded books
that unlock windows,
breezes of insights
blowing justice

to change the questions
every heart requests
answers to, loving
hands rebuilding
everything.

Outside Church

Angry white lady
with a bible
hates us in church,
behind smiles
planning manipulation
of our futures.

Outside,
an unhoused man
stocks canned goods
in a free pantry,
talking to himself,
then telling us
to have a good day.

Not Your Black People

Despite rainbow flags
waving outside church,
you have no right
to claim my spouse
and three beautiful children
as your own.

They are not your Black people.
They are their own.

Why did you tell
Black church visitors
you usually had Black people,
present and attending,
referring to my family?

They are not your Black people.
They are their own.

These visitors smiled,
looked me in the eye
with a knowing look,
something like
rageful sympathy,
then never returned, because

They are not your Black people.
They are their own.

My family does not exist
as some badge of honor
for you to wear,

attempting to impress others
with your goodness,
inclusiveness, progress.

They are not your Black people.
They are their own

Not Up to You

You don't get to decide
when words hurt,
and actions harm,
that we shouldn't be
so upset, so angry,
so quick to say
it is not alright.

You are not the judge
of when something
is racist, bigoted,
transphobic, homophobic,
ableist, fatphobic,
or harmful in myriad ways.

Intention and impact
are not always the same.
Your tears are swords
and we disallow you
the power required
to make us feel crazy
today, tomorrow, or ever.

Reflective Pause: Self-Loyalty

"Not Up to You" touches on themes of gaslighting, personal agency, and boundaries, emphasizing the importance of trusting ourselves and our perceptions, especially as individuals holding multiple marginalized identities. Over the years, I cannot count the number of times I have exerted emotional labor to call someone in and explain how our family has been harmed, only to find myself on the receiving end of disbelief, anger, rage, or manipulative tears. As the white member of our family, this most often happens when I find myself in conversation with other white people. Yet, I still speak up because if I do not, who will?

As you read, I invite you to reflect on the significance of finding and using your own voice, especially if you feel that it has often been silenced, excluded, distrusted, or disbelieved. Gaslighting is a manipulative behavior where another person attempts to make you doubt your own experiences and perceptions. Trusting your feelings and intuition in the face of this is vital to maintaining your personal well-being, agency, and healthy boundaries. You get to stand firm in your understanding of what is right and wrong, without seeking permission from those who have hurt you or those you love. When you affirm your own embodied truth, it helps to create space for healing and empowerment, protecting your peace in ways that create social change.

Reflective Writing Exercise

Reflect on a time when someone who hurt you tried to invalidate your feelings or experiences. How did it feel, and did you recognize the dynamics at play immediately, or did it take some time? Next, think of a time when you successfully used your voice to validate your own experiences and establish needed boundaries. If you are still struggling to do this for yourself, imagine what it might feel like to be the person equipped with the tools needed for self-advocacy. Where could you find support for this area of personal growth?

Write a poem that explores the emotions and the strength required to trust yourself, maintain your boundaries, and use your voice. Consider sharing this poem with someone close to you or in a space where it is likely to inspire others with similar lived experiences.

Not the Same

I was mistaken
when I thought
maybe we could be
friends.

Interracial couples,
raising little kids
in rural areas, but
we are not the same.

My family never
hated my spouse
for his Blackness,

and our religion
never led us
to colonize
Muslim friends,

reject queerness,
or beat our children
for daring to have
minds of their own.

First Baby Lost

Your fluttering heartbeat
birthed me, parent,
daring me to believe
in the possibility of little feet
after months of trying
with only negatives.

One ectopic life ended
with surgery, chemo,
and me waking wailing,
mourning each morning
until another soul came along.
But, your life brought me love.

Boxing Day

5am water breaks,
Lucas born lifeless.
Dingy motel floor,
his brother plays.
I pray for playmates.

I live to hope,
to grieve, to plan,
to bury you with songs,
little baby booties,
a blanket, and our love.

Alone

Grieving alone,
toddler plays
happily at my feet.
I clutch my gut,
clawing emptiness.
He is gone.
A week ago, you said,
"I will sit with you.
Be there at noon."
It is six o'clock.

Trying to find
reasons to live,
I breathe breaths
one at a time,
wondering whether
anyone recognizes,
knows the effort required
to stay alive when baby
did not.

Nearly seven o'clock
you pull up the drive,
hand me a stack
of gift cards,
informing me
you had errands to run.
Thankfully, my spouse
comes home.

Abortion

Saved my life
through heartbreak
for lives lost,
dreams abandoned,
hope left longing,
and doctors declaring
devastation through
tears, knowing love
was waiting here
in these empty arms.

Is my choice,
my doctor's choice,
for giving futures
to my children
who need my
bleeding to stop,
so I can
tie their shoes,
make soup,
walk in the park,
read them a book.

Is healthcare,
human rights,
my spouse's longing
to kiss me tonight
rather than bury
my ashes
in a grave,
telling the children
this happened because

politicians impersonate
physicians.

The Last Baby

Four months pregnant,
bleeding attempts murder.
Surgery and transfusions
save rapidly draining life
from red puddles,
shattered, broken dreams.

I mourn my last baby.

Three children complain
in daddy's worried arms,
smiling as I wake up.
Wave hello to little eyes,
but goodbye to baby years,
and all that could have been.

Poverty

Poverty is more palatable
when it does not smile
on mountainsides,
weave wondrous
words, with multiple
degrees on the wall,
eat salads by lakes,
photograph beauty,
laugh boisterously,
read literature,
present cleanly,
put together style,
play with children,
snuggle with pets,
dance in diversity,
thrive in joy,
or look like me,
which looks like you,
making food banks,
food stamps,
Medicaid,
negative balances,
and financial ruin
hit too close to home.

Failure

Failure means centering
me, you, them, or your friend,
instead of intentionally,
bravely, boldly, profoundly
meeting the self-voiced needs
of the most marginalized,
whose paths open the way
for the rest of us
in the process.

Excluded

Facebook glitters
with smiling photos,
my children's
white dance friends
and birthday cake,
singing, petting farm
goats, with a stack
of shiny new presents.
Missing? My children,
their mocha brown
skin, big hearts,
and sweet laugher,
their belief,
still persisting,
that most people
are loving, kind,
fair, and honest.
My kids stack
Legos, with crayons
and paper nearby,
Cheerios in cups,
as Minecraft YouTube
lights up a screen.
They were
the only ones
not invited.

Burnout

Burnt-out
lead heavy legs,
brain numb,
emotions worn down,
dead inside,
rendered useless
plans made.
Unsustainable
coping, pretending
worlds thrive,
fake smiles beaming
after bigotry flies
on flags, the world
rotating normally.
Longing barely
whispers its begging
for nourishment,
indulgence
of every kind.

Service Dog Access

Where are
her papers?
Only
certified
service dogs
allowed.

Certification
doesn't exist,
ADA requires
access, see
this law.

White woman
scowls, wants
to pet
my service dog.
She's working.

Doesn't believe
me or my
three Black kids,
as panic and rage
ruin enjoyment
of the tulips.

Trump Signs

Eleven Trump signs
line our rural road,
welcome signs
for hate
on morning walks.

We are not
welcome here,
but we smile,
wave, and

notice no
Mark Robinson
signs signaling
Nazi, slave-wanting,
pedophilia harboring
sentiments,
like that highway
in the mountains.

Capitol Pride Picnic

D.C. green,
sandwiches, waters,
blessed rest.
Smiles, laughter,
joy, freedom
at last.

White man,
neo-Nazi
dressed in black,
eyes glaring hate.
Feeling hunted
haunts the air.

Tired

Tired of
hopping nonstop,
burning bright,
toiling in fright
of catastrophe
in breaking,

need a break
from Instagramming,
programming
swirling, twirling,
demanding change
from deranged
worlds of hate.

Dreary doldrums
drain desire,
running down,
letting down,
inner children
crying

for restoration,
affirmation,
nourishment,
boundaries,
freedom,
overflowing
abundance

of self-care,
community-care,
where we share

in dances, books,
walks, movement,
nature, peace,
reigniting spark
for life.

Anything but Cancer

Prayers stream down
my cheeks, begging,
pleading, demanding,
anything but cancer,
even if she is strong,
fierce, capable, free.
I can't let it be,
help me, Amabie,
emerge from the sea,
bathing our being
in divine radiance
for the road ahead.

Cancer Again

Brokenhearted grief
on our bed again
as cancer crashes
the party wickedly,
crushing us in loss,
while souls forget
perhaps goodness waits
on the other side
of this strange,
unexplored land,
where not all is lost
to scalpels, and
blessedly Black
doctors see
humanity and love,
hoping clover
has our backs,
expanding love
and chances
for a future.

Panicked Awake

"No!!," I screamed,
eyes jolting awake,
heart racing,
stomach sinking,
gloom looming,
dread schooling,
until relief washes
tears from my eyes.

Dear body
trying to keep me safe,
the cancer
has not returned,
but I am glad
you remembered.

White Hospital

Everyone except him
is privileged, white.
So are the walls, floors,
these harsh lights
assaulting senses,
with disinfectant,
smells of sickness,
and lack of masks
on everyone's faces
except ours.

Text message:
"Daddy will be okay,"
figures rushing,
gazes avoiding,
helping others,
while my love's deep
brown eyes and skin
sit unattended,
cold hard chair,
monitors beeping,
refusing to back up
my claims.

Reflective Pause: Inequity

"White Hospital" addresses racist healthcare inequity and medical neglect, especially in healthcare settings where privilege and systemic biases are most obvious, such as in the predominantly white rural hospital where my spouse was taken via ambulance in 2023. Even though he was in immense pain and having trouble breathing, he was still on the receiving end of poor care. As you read, I encourage you to reflect on inequity, invisibility, advocacy, and the emotional toll of navigating spaces where you or someone you care about might find themselves othered.

Invisibility, inequity, and othering in healthcare settings can result in negative health impacts, emotional trauma, or even death. Learning to advocate for ourselves and our loved ones is lifesaving and helps increase the odds that everyone receives the care and attention they deserve. This often means exerting a great deal of emotional labor to challenge the status quo repeatedly and persistently, demanding equity in spaces that were not built to affirm us or our loved ones. Addressing both immediate needs and systemic changes helps create the needed social change to ensure greater equity in the long run.

Reflective Writing Exercise

Reflect on a time when you or a loved one was harmed in a space where privilege and systemic biases or racism were evident. How did this experience feel, what steps did you take, or wish you had taken, to advocate for yourself or your loved one? What is it like to exert that level of emotional labor during times of crisis? What systemic changes would make this exertion less necessary?

Write a poem exploring the emotional labor required to navigate and challenge systemic injustice and inequity. Consider sharing this poem with someone close to you or in a space where it might inspire others to seek social change.

Be Safe

Be safe
the night
of our child's
birthday,
when water
sends your truck
spinning,

a white lady
swerves,
totaling her
Audi,
then says
she'd have to
trust you
not to drive off
if you wait
in your car.

Be safe
when the cops
are on the way,
the kids and I
gathering around
our kitchen table,
waiting to hear
you are still
coming home
tonight,

me hoping
I won't have to
tell our kid

about fatal
racism
on her birthday,
interrupting her
everything.

Dear Son

If the cops
pull you over,
record and
text me.
Believe me,
I will be there,
magically becoming,
transforming into
a white woman,
voice and mannerisms,
the whole shebang,
dysphoria be damned,
so maybe you
will not
become gone.

Layoffs

Our turn for layoffs.
We understand
how hardship
calls opportunity
from pain's gutters,
discouragement
fearfully forgetting
how our efforts
count regardless.

What if we
honestly intuit
doubts and promise,
head and heart
hungering for some
hope of Babalu Aye,
weaving fevers from earth,
brooms sweeping through
our home with healing?

No Boundaries

The nerve
to assume
a stranger
you just met
wants to discuss
intimate,
play-by-play
details of
oral sex
and your
boyfriend,

or tell you how
sex works
with someone
of another gender,
a trans person.

Where does everyone
put their hands,
mouths, body parts?
Would you ask
these questions
of a straight person?

Concerned for Your Health

Pretty for a big girl,
not slender,
such a lovely face,
so brave to wear
those crop tops
and bike shorts,
but never to church.
Wouldn't that be
obscene?

Don't take this
the wrong way.
I'm concerned for
your health.
Not so many snacks.
Have an apple,
an orange,
some broccoli,
take a walk.

Now watch me
obsess over
diet books
until all
you eat today
and tomorrow
is a salted pretzel
secretly thrown up
in the bathroom,
wanting to die.

Fatphobia

Your fatphobia
is not flattering,
especially when
you talk about
your diet,
the latest
weight loss
injections
that paralyze
your stomach,
your surgery,
the o-word slur,
or how fat
and gross
your legs were
while pregnant.

Your fatphobia
makes your
evil show
when you
shame children
for eating
apples and
peanut butter,
or tell trans folx
they must
lose weight
before top surgery
is an option,
moments later
offering to amputate
their stomachs.

Your fatphobia
is racism
when BMI charts
have a sordid
history,
cereal too,
and you know
nothing of
"Fearing the
Black Body."

Again, your fatphobia
is not flattering.
Have you ever
considered losing it?

Not a Pervert

Second grade,
girlfriends explore
closeness,
but adults interfere,
shame us,
until we conclude
we are bad, wrong.
Never again.

Sixth grade,
she declares
bisexual people
perverts,
just wanting to
fuck everybody.
Not a pervert.
Can't be me.

Eighth grade,
gay or straight,
she doesn't hate,
so we debate,

(my friends and I)

who we'd rather kiss,
and declare
we must be straight
because it means
no more hate
as long as we remain
virgins.

Agreeing to Disagree

Agreeing to disagree
means accepting
my family's annihilation
in 500 anti-trans bills,
and your deeply held conviction
that we are going to hell,
lost, in need of Jesus,
as you prepare to vote
for someone asserting
that some people
just need killing,
maybe including us.

Your Hate

Your hate
still rings the same,
your destruction
doesn't change.
Different face,
different name,
disruptions
came with flame.

Hate is Still Hate

Hate covered in honey
is still hate.
Religion saying,
love the sinner
hate the sin,
is still hate.

When hate
visits trauma,
let your heart break,
let your tears come,
let your anger rise,
let your body
hold it no more,

as soul friends
hold space for devastation,
loving wholeheartedly.

Listen

Dear cishet,
liberal
white folx,
would you please
stop the
pontificating,
self-important
diatribes,
intellectual,
philosophical
debates and
microaggressions
about things you have
no lived experience
navigating for survival?

What if,
instead,
you grew silent,
intentionally,
long enough
to center,
to deeply hear,
voices of folx
who live it daily,
listening,
passing torches
with humility,
amends, commitment,
action,
respect,
and admiration?

Not All

"Not all religious people..."
"Not all white people..."
"Not all cis people..."
"Not all police..."
But what about you?
Will you responsibly stop it?
Why not amplify,
center voices brave
enough, daring enough,
vulnerable enough
to uncover raw wounds
and say the hard part out loud,
rather than silencing
how we fail to understand
religious people who
"love everyone"
yet hate others because
they love them (?!?),
especially when they are
queer, or trans, interracial,
Black, Brown, or Indigenous,
Immigrant, poor, fat, disabled,
or anything not thin, cishet, white,
Christian, moneyed, or you.
Especially when allowing
our voices might cost you.

Cult

begins with
questioning,
assuming
my perceptions
have always
been wrong,

tumbling into
upside down
living, fear
preventing
escape,
until one day,

your hate
reveals you
have always
seen Blackness,
Queerness,
Fatness,
as less than
human,
and primed them
for your exploits.

No

You do not
lead my life,
with uninvited
fatphobia,
transphobia,
homophobia,
classism,
and fucked up hate.

No!
I clutch
my reins,
decisiveness
protecting,
persistence
blazing bright trails
demanding change,

refusing
anything less
than affirming winds
for every life,
and soul,
with breath.

Bone Tired

Tired of melanin challenged,
cishet, bone thin males
trying to own identities,
and speak
about experiences
like intellectual exercises
between their ears,
without their hearts,
because they have never,
not once,
experienced in blood
and bones
what living is like
in bodies that know
how it feels
to be hunted.

Life and Survival

are difficult to balance
when trauma reigns
with thunder,
growing louder, scarier
with each news cycle,
and bank accounts
growing slimmer
with each day
of grueling work
that's better spent
making cake
or playing in pools
with smiling children,
the same ones
facing bigotry and risk
with every venture
out the front door,
and every time
good hearted people
refuse to vote
for brighter sunshine,
in favor of giving up.

Not Getting the Job

Before the email,
"pursue another candidate,"
my heart knows,
knocks on the door,
crushes hopes with reality,
bare pantries, empty accounts,
hungry mouths, inadequacy,
queerness, disability,
and melanated family
below the Mason-Dixon line,
where second chances at success
are drowned by seas of
Trump signs, confederate flags,
and covered up lynchings,
proclaiming existence
dangerous here.

Passive Aggressive White Women

I have voice and
white women grow silent
when highlighting bigotry
breaks and brakes their codes
of niceties, smiles, and illusions
that everything about them
is lovely, delicate, good.

They are done with me,
my "sensitivity," wokeness,
my meanness, aggressiveness,
scared of what I might know,
yet have zero ounces of courage
to tell me to my face.

Dear Allies

Actions,
not thoughts,
not prayers,
not you're so brave,
make worlds
where suffering
is not assumed,
worlds where
existence is affirmed

so we catch breaths,
take another, and another,
finding respite in sunshine,
trees and fresh air,
safe enough to savor
when the battle
is not ours alone.
Allies believe, listen,
take action.

Schoolhouse Questions

Who would I be
if school
had been safe
to be fat,
queer,
trans,
poor,
autistic,
different
numerously, yet
affirmed
instead of
bullied?

What would I have
learned, if learning
had been
about books,
not surviving
lunchroom taunts,
teachers who
laugh at
"fatso,"
adults believing
different is to be
eradicated?

What would I earn
if I had learned
from books
where money
comes from,
been given

permission
to request pay
for labor
that makes a
difference
instead of told
to go away?

Unraveling Therapy

Seven years
and therapy crumbles,
wisdom and strength
wisely illuminating
exclusion,
resilience offering lifelines
when a therapist's
bigotry blows through.

Paralysis evaporates,
fiercely soulful certainty
assuring younger parts
of freedom to abandon
spaces vetoing rainbows,
especially now.

Tangled in knots,
barbed threads abandoned,
citrine quartz uncovered,
self-worth gleaming,
shining deep knowing:
Affirmation is oxygen for life.

Goodbyes and soul progress
bring tears of relief,
that confidence has settled
into belief that we are worthy
of equitable healing,
affirming horizons. Safety.

Self-Defense for Kids

It says something
when self-defense class
feels like hope,
relief, possibility,
in the face of bathrooms,
religious zealots,
and voting booths.

Can we find no better
way to live freely
than offering children
skills to save lives
that some call slurs
but we call
our entire hearts?

Go child,
learn today,
to defend your life today,
as I fight today,
try to create today,
worlds where self-defense
classes are not our hope
for life.

J.D. Vance

Queer hating
white men
do not
represent me,
my heart,
my family,
especially on
the worst of days,
when raining
anti-trans bills
from clouded skies
threaten our existence,

yet we refuse to cave,
instead birthing
decisive, courageous
action,
poems reflecting
culture,
intentionally alienating
anti-human rights
characters from shadows,

protests born
of love and voice,
voting booth choices
from conviction,
even when we
fear the mob
that wanted
violence last time,
and wonder

if our choices
matter at all.

J.K. Rowling

Candle lit,
soft piano
lulling my soul
to let go
of the harsh
winds of worlds
unkind.

Safety invites
vulnerability,
walls releasing,
pen ready to write
words I have
shared with
no one,

and then,

J.K. Rowling's
name falls
from your lips,
an illustration
in writing,
pouring salt
on rawness
newly unzipped,

transphobia
erasing every
word I nearly
released
in spaces

never built
for me,
but I know you
mean well.

Waiting for Service

Honey, let us be seen.
Let the twinkle in our eyes
spread joy like sunlight,
oceans of delight,
love more than alright.

Worn tables, wafting smells,
rumbling bellies, dating diners,
bustling restaurant vibes
exciting connection, delection,
flirtatious laughter with you.

Your beautiful brown skin,
my splotchy sunburned shoulders,
as we wait...and wait
while white women eat,
and nobody takes our order.

Service denied, throats dense,
hearts raging, blood cursing,
mouths polite, wallets tight
keeping composure,
we leave.

Resilience

is overrated,
oversold,
and forgets
one simple truth:

We are not meant
to be better at
being oppressed.

If we were,
what point
would there be
in seeking justice?

PART II: COMPLEXITY

"Only by learning to live in harmony with your contradictions can you keep it all afloat."

— AUDRE LORDE, *PARADE*

THOUGHTS ON COMPLEXITY

ALICE WALKER SAID, "HARD TIMES REQUIRE FURIOUS dancing. Each of us is proof.[1]" My family has found that even in the hardest times, there are usually moments of joy to hang onto, fueling us forward toward brighter days. I am most dramatically reminded of the time I gave birth to a baby on Christmas Eve while my mother was across the state, and in the days-long process of dying. New life and joy sustained me during that time of loss, giving me a reason to get up and celebrate life each morning. Sometimes, it takes more intentional and determined effort to find and hold onto joy in the midst of our storms, like the time that my family rejoiced in an entire case of perfectly fresh raspberries from the food pantry, just as we ran out of fruit to eat.

At the same time, when times feel more easily joyful, elements of deep grief or trauma can still run as quiet undercurrents in our lives. Being aware of them is key to ensuring that peace and love also remain present. For instance, the writing and publication of this book has brought me great joy, yet many of the family members I wish I could share it with have relatively recently passed on. As I type this, I am wearing a "Somewhere Over the

---

1. *Walker, Alice. Hard Times Require Furious Dancing: New Poems. New World Library, 2013, p. 12.*

Rainbow" t-shirt, reminiscing about the many lazy afternoons I spent listening to that song on the back deck with my Grandpa, who died at the age of 102, near the end of 2022. Life is complex. The poems in this section embrace that reality and run with it.

Choosing to embrace the complexity of our lives is one way that those of us holding multiple marginalized identities can reclaim a sense of empowerment and agency. Honestly recognizing the complex dynamics and emotions at play in our daily lives means that we are freed up to tend to what we truly want and need, rather than merely meeting our obligations and taking care of responsibilities. In the process, we might even address our self-limiting beliefs, internalized oppression, privileges, and any unhelpful inner voices that have kept us from dancing *our* way through the ups and downs of life. We learn to trust ourselves, following our own internal compasses, while choosing unconditional love above all else.

After all, we cannot do any more to stop the pain of life than we can to stop a hurricane destined to pass over our homes while we evacuate or shelter in place. What we can do is choose to love others and ourselves while the storm passes and as we recover from it. We can learn to connect meaningfully instead of pulling away due to fear, balancing our need for vulnerability with our need for protection and care. Believing we are worthy of that care means that we begin noticing glimmers of gratitude and opportunities for delight, even during trying times. We learn to feed ourselves with words of appreciation, love, and affirmation that nourish not only us but the communities around us as well.

Garden Reprieve

After the long day,
when she, in her whiteness,
advised raising children
in Aunt Jemima's likeness,
destroying "friendship" instantly,
my feet hit warm garden soil,
sweat beading in my hair,
sun kissing my shoulders,
as heirloom tomatoes beckon,
while lips taste hot peppers,
noses smell roses,
and children frolic boisterously
in joyful sprinkler water.

Create Goodness

When hope
extinguishes
its last flames,
create goodness
with tomatoes,
garlic, peppers,
cilantro, honey,
love growing
in broth simmering
something more
than giving up.

My Words Matter

because many isolate
in Southern rural
homes,
feeling like
islands
in seas of white
evangelical Christianity,
the only marginalized
families enduring
bullshit because bigots
stake their claim
as sovereign heirs
to beautiful places,

yet we remain,
enduring, enjoying,
taking up space,
believing if
diversity leaves,
they get what
they want, and
it will never, ever
be safer here

for rainbows of
every kind,
diversities innumerable
who enjoy, crave, savor
living on land
with cricket songs,
rows of tomatoes,
tall tree forests,
and birds of every kind,

so my words matter,
and if you are nodding,
your heart relates,
you're out here, too,
and so do you.

Queer Homeschool

Safe havens
make learning
possible,
when othering
withers, as welcome
affirms humanity
in history, not banned,

and empowerment
means you are
perfect
just
as
you
are,
even on tough days,

and this refuge
prepares you to
say no to bullies,
leave unsafe spaces,
stand up for love,
follow your dreams,
have your consent
and your boundaries
respected,

so you grow strong
into world-changing,
people-adoring,
everyone-including,
alive, equipped
you.

Reflective Pause: Education

"Queer Homeschool" highlights what it is like to create safe, equitable, and affirming spaces for children who would likely be unsafe in their local public schools due to holding multiple marginalized identities in spaces where that is not the norm. As you read, I invite you to reflect on the tragedy of these realities, the urgent need for better funding for public schools, increased support for teachers, systems that support equity, as well as the importance of an inclusive and affirming education that teaches all of history without banning books that amplify marginalized voices.

My family chooses to homeschool our three children for the reasons outlined above, and we have occasionally faced criticism from well-meaning cishet, middle or upper middle class white liberals who tell our children that their favorite part of school was seeing all their friends every day. They hype school up as a marvelous experience but often fail to recognize that their schools were mostly filled with other cishet white kids who shared very similar societal lived experiences and social locations. School is an entirely different experience for queer, racialized children with multiple marginalized identities in predominantly white, cishet environments, where they are not free to leave or set strong boundaries when injustice visits them.

For these reasons, we have found that safe havens are key to making learning accessible for children who face othering and exclusion in predominantly white, cishet school environments. While my spouse and I educate our kids at home, they meet friends in other spaces and places, such as through the queer community center in the nearest big city to us, vetted online groups, and community activities. These environments affirm their humanity and provide a refuge where they can grow and thrive, while honoring their agency, boundaries, and consent. The need for our approach underscores the failures of our government to adequately fund and support our public education system in ways that ensure a safe and inclusive environment for all students.

Reflective Writing Exercise

Imagine being a child who feels unsafe in their school setting due to othering, but who is not allowed to leave because they are a minor. How might this experience impact their ability to learn and thrive, both emotionally and intellectually? What changes might make the school environment more inclusive and supportive?

Write a poem that calls for increased equity in the education system, focusing on the emotional experiences of children. Consider the impact of better funding, intentional hiring practices, and systemic changes that support equity. If you feel comfortable, share this poem on social media or with representatives who have the power to help enact positive change.

Together Forward

Take my hand
in this sorrow of
hardship, loss
sadness, injustice.
Below stars,
we limp, canes
bearing hard times,
help nourishing,
step by step,
soul wisdom
heartfully
empowering
expression where
waiting loves
rejoice, relieved.

Transformation

Let transformation come,
especially when hopelessness
threatens to cage your soul
with surrender to misery,
heavy loads and injustice.

Let things fall apart,
glue dissolving, crumbling
every piece, shattered
to be reassembled
in radiant newness.

Interracial

Adjective,
when two races
are connected,
in our case,
in love.

Misperceptions:
fetishized,
unstable,
uneducated,
unwanted,
unsupported,
recent trend,
a threat,
straight.

In reality,
we choose
each other
lovingly,
bravely,
no matter
what happens
out there.

Rest Softly

Rest softly
as pain melts into
unconditional love,
soul rejuvenating,
restoring peace,
even in the midst
of hate.

Rest kindly,
inspiration and guidance
(like cookies)
offers sweet synchronicities,
refreshing every part of you,
healing leading the way.

Soar

College calls
while I smile,
tears in my eyes,
ready to
watch you soar.

Childhood is
fastly fleeting,
with its
video games,
playgrounds,
jammy days,
and birthdays,
where I see you
like the moment
you were born.

This lump in
my throat,
these tear-stained
cheeks are in
gratitude
for having been
chosen to
be your home,

watching you
spread wings,
grasping dreams,
with all the
wonder you
had in learning
to read.

Intersectional

And...
interracial family
AND some of us
are queer,
trans,
Black,
Indigenous,
white,
fat,
disabled,
poor,
homeschooled,
degreed,
engineers,
writers,
homeowners,
unemployed,
neuro-geeks,
artists,
programmers,
service-dog handlers,
college bound,
gardeners,
business owners,
loving,
kind,
passionate,
determined,
resourceful,
spiritual,
together,
AND it is never

OR,
always and,
yet so much more.

Watch Me

Despite nightmares
of imprisonment and death,
and a day with threats of violence,
attempted refusal of service,
coupled with disgust and bigotry,

I am becoming, claiming,
thriving wildly and splashing in
everything I wish to be,
as my existence topples towers,

my very breath ending old ways,
ushering change with jubilation,
in the face of bigoted tantrums
and denials of history,

flying in the face of norms,
inviting transformation incrementally,
communities intersecting mosaically,
with colorfully defiant beauty,
affirming our joyfully dancing souls.

Whisperjourney

Whisper,
Journey,
Whisperjourney:
fertile foundation
where quiet labor
secretly sprouts seeds
within the heart,
tended with care,
patience, love,
and root stimulator,
resulting in surprise
abundance,
splendor blooming
everywhere.

Loving Whisperjourney

Interracial love:
Illegal.
Mildred and Richard:
Married and arrested,
a.r.r.e.s.t.e.d.
for loving, even
with the last name
Loving.

Virginia bars them—
nine years in D.C.,
harrowing fight,
Mildred persisting,
Cohen assisting,
Richard loved
his wife.

Supreme Court,
June 12, 1967,
Loving Day,
our marriage made
legal,
whisperjourney,
mere decades in
advance of our
first kiss.

Our Mosaic Hearts

originate from
whisperjourneys,
loving and
Loving,
Black folx
marching,
Indigenous folx
daring,
Norwegian folx
adventuring

boldly,
risks taken,
sacrifices made,
fights won,
bare feet,
toes wiggling
in freshly cut
grass,
babies birthing,
parents singing,
ovens baking,

hands writing,
minds inventing,
souls demanding
more than
equality,
more than
inclusion,
every bit of
affirmation

High Priestess
Isis
and Gramme's
Green Man
enchanted
for the garden
of our hearts,
effortlessly
flowering,
blossoming boldly,
in grand magnificence
of nature.

No Money

Yet words live,
breathing delight
this silent night,
soothing routines
like ocean brine,
balancing mind,
body, spirit,

equilibrium
connecting self
and universes of
calm, soulful
thoughts, dissolving
worries in deep
breaths abundantly.

Attention Shoppers

Attention shoppers:
Effective immediately,
I am welcoming new risk
and disposing of old uniforms,
as clamoring doubt and fear
are no longer welcome here.

In every isle,
I am now liberated
from solid plans,
swinging freely on
love strings of my heart,
spawning giddy delight,
head thrown back in the wind,
refueling on genuine laughter within.

Blessing

May wisdom and peace
bubble to overflowing
with wellsprings of comfort,
protection from harm,
hands of healing,
hearts of hope,
and serenity quieting fear.

May clarity illuminate
verdant paths of purpose,
justice washing suffering,
resolutely bold action
with compassion, inclusion
raining from rainbows:
We breathe freely everywhere.

Just in Case

Just in case
things fall apart,
I have this cash,
those cards,
some electrolytes
for fainting,
dark chocolate
for blood sugar,
hand sanitizer
for germs,
chapstick
for chapped lips,
hand cream
for dry hands,
epi-pens
for lifesaving,
keys
for self-defense,
napkins
for messes,
love and hope
for when the world
says nope.

She Tried to Crush Me

Yet I retrieve
my power
as my own,
blindfold removed,
limits crushed,
eyes open,
fire ignited,
asserting worth,
intrinsic,
purposeful
momentum,
goodness
unstoppable.
Confidence,
not pretending.

Life's Complexity

Life's depth is measured in richness,
not plateaus or avoided storms.
Look honestly to peaks and falls,
oceans and volcanoes,
beyond thinness in love and joy,
comfort and ease, alone.
Life's lows echo in night skies,
deep canvases showcasing brilliance,
glistening shooting stars,
dancing northern lights
enchanting captivating flames,
inspiring delight through the night.

Lost

I have lost my way,
my hope, my love,
my faith,
and sight of the future,
and then lost my will,
my drive, my belief,
my self-worth,
and my purpose,
but then found
my anger,
boiling rage,
fiery voice,
feet with mission,
causing me to
lose all my fucks,
my desire to please,
the masks hiding
true feelings and needs,
uncovering piles
and piles of leaves,
only to find me.

Rural Queer Interracial Life

means no bumper stickers
or yard signs,
rainbow flags flying,
Black Lives Matter
merch of all kinds,
outside the house,
where people might
find us, harass us,
hurt us, target us.

It also means
embracing t-shirts,
(political)
publishing books,
attending rallies with
voices unfiltered,
to squash hate with love,
while chili simmers,
made with home canned
tomatoes, peppers,
green beans, pintos,
spices, and dreams
of s'mores, campfires

and more privileged,
less vulnerable families
brave enough
to hang the flags,
set the signs,
decorate their homes
with love so that
one day, we are free
to do the same.

Kamala

She is confetti,
so much more than
merely a cog
or supporting cast member,
as you reduce her
to a white man's record.

She is generations
of my children's ancestors,
wrapped in pink and green,
radiating power,
genius, resourcefulness,
confident assurance
that every single thing
is still possible.

Improvement

waves hello,
as an elderly
white woman
sporting blue hair,
a Duke blue shirt,
and pearls

spots my Kamala
campaign t-shirt,
erupting in joy
to inquire if we
are registered
to vote,
our friends, too,

declaring young people
(I'm in my 40's)
the answer, the way,
the path to
brighter days
past orange haze,
and impending doom.

Hope After Hate

Reishi mushrooms
ladder up dead hemlocks,
reminders that death
brings new life.
Hatred sows loss,
but love inoculates
abounding affirmation
as we hike mountains,
base to summit,
lakes to meadows,
wildflowers dancing,
leaping joyfully as we go.

Hands

Strong hands,
spotted and wrinkled,
caring, supporting
life gleefully.
They tied shoes,
canned peaches,
made bread,
carried radios
in WWII,
tilled soil,
harvested fruit,
wrapped presents,
steered bicycles,
heated soup,
played ball,
hugged firmly,
and wrote
"I love you"
on cards—
remaining pieces
of you.

Unforgotten

Unforgotten is your love,
or final embrace:
"Beautiful family.
Just beautiful!
You have so much
to look forward to."
"Best Grandpa ever."

Leaving, feet disconnected
from heart, cemented
with eternal goodbyes,
tears watering love.
I wanted to stay
where your hand still held

my heart on earth.
I hoped you were right
about a bright future.
For your sake,
we drove home,
wondering what next.

Winter Waters Spring

Winter's softly quiet
internal snow
finally releases drips
to seeds waiting, dormant
beneath fertile soil,
where hope felt futile,
until cyan tendrils

burst bravely toward
heartening spring's light,
nourished in rested soil,
old things dissolved.
Fresh possibilities
sing of delicate radiance,
good things to come.

Accepting Help

When the cupboards
are nearly bare,
accepting help
is success,
is welcoming
abundance again,
when you gift others
joy in loving you
through apples,
kale, cabbage,
and juicy cases
of fresh raspberries.

Accepting help
is success,
not some failure
at being
marginalized
without complaining
or draining, burdening.
You are drawing from
the same reserves of joy
grown in love,
scattered in the wind
for decades,
you have given others.

Welcoming Tears

Follow warm teardrops
falling from the heart's
overwhelmed blossoms,

Brokenhearted love
bursts within them,
for every soul in need

of safety, protection,
human rights, freedom
to exist fully, to dance

in showers of rainbow's
teardrops turned to
joyful jubilation, as

justice rains down:
metamorphosis, dreams.

Worthy

You, too, are worthy
of moments invested
by people admired,
personal connection,
time, interest,
good happenings,
sparkling affirmation
breaking draughts

with runes
whispering truths,
symmetrically sowing
peace, inspiring
risk toward fulfilling
futures fought
and won in love.

Trans Day of Visibility

Plea in pulses of goodness,
open hearts dancing,
demanding and chanting,
acting and hasting,
seeing seas of souls:

pink/white/blue,
pure promise and pride,
worthy of wonder,
of dancing, no thunder,
of peaceful pauses,
exhaling when worlds

level hate, ignite roars
of inclusion, opening
clearings, safe havens,
and finally existence
promenades with permanence.

Unlimited

Gorgeous soul,
magnificent and beautiful,
every dream on your heart
is possible, probable,
no matter how hard,
how filthy, how sweaty,
the grueling climb
to panoramic views
where mirrors offer
splendid views
of the most lovable you.
Keep climbing.

Superhero

You are
your own superhero,
special and unique,

shining love fearlessly,
embracing others
boldly and authentically,

magnificently gifting
talents generously,
energy abundantly

propelling you
toward the pleasure
and delight of your heart.

Love is the Easy Part

She is wrong. Our love
is not calamity and loss
by virtue of who we are.
Bigotry offers sour tantrums,
while love is succulent and sweet.

Our love is a warm blanket
on a cold winter's night.
This love is goodness and grace,
small delights by candlelight,
and shelter from the storm.

Our love is a safe landing place,
cotton candy at the carnival,
ocean walks and mountain tops,
comforting arms, a gentle embrace.
Release now, backdrops of hate,
our love is the easy part.

Safe Spaces

Necessitate boundaries,
knowing capacity
limits empathy
for privileged tears
from identities
who harm by
existing.

Say no
in compassion
when emotions,
hot tears,
know encouragement
flies with swallows
in protection.

Inner Wolf Rising

My inner wolf rises
with lion-like roar,
forging new paths,
protecting tender hearts,
opening glimmering roads:
authenticity and courage.

Two young wolves gathering
young brave souls,
rainbows woven for good
warding off hate,
cozying dens of peace.
You are safe here.

You are seen here.
You are loved here.
You are welcome here.
You are affirmed here.
We find hope here.
Together here, we thrive.

Ripples Emerging

Ripples meet
where pain wails
longingly for connection,
hope, nurture, healing
beyond calm waters
laden with isolation,
and muted voices.

Ripples spark
heart-focused radiation,
igniting purpose,
tender hands that hold,
hearts that heal,
tears that cleanse

toward healing boldly,
swimming in purpose:
together, not alone.
In schools of love,
propelled by delight,
as ripples converge,
wholeness emerges, radiant.

Office Magic

These four walls
welcome my fatness,
queerness, poorness,
pain, sorrow, rage
in a sea of Trump signs.

Respite here
as walls crumble,
offering rawness,
trauma needing healing,
hope for brighter days,

until power surges
in whirlwinds of love,
removing obstacles,
clearing circles of purpose
where we dance freely,

flames of determination,
strength, deep roars
honoring ancestors,
clearing the way
for children to come.

Dare Believe

In the face of it all,
dare believe
magical power
embeds your dreams,
waves released,
healing worlds wildly,
when whispers wonder,
wandering wakefully,
wistfully, wishfully,
wokefully, wonderfully,
spellfully singing swiftly
so willfully hands, feet,
hearts, minds, souls,
serenade, sparking
serenity. Someone
sails, survives, thrives.

You Matter

Child, heart of mine:
your life matters
in every city, school,
bathroom, and corner
bullies want to steal.
My breath shouts it.

Your life is a gift
of radiant rainbows,
overflowing love,
brilliant stars innumerable,
treasures mysterious.
Look in my tearful eyes...

You are worthy of the universe,
of protection, justice, love,
care and kindness,
the chance to grow up.
this world is better because
your breath is in it.

Love, Mom

Reflective Pause: Protect Trans Kids

"You Matter" explores the emotions and dangers often faced by trans and gender expansive youth and their families, while radically affirming their inherent worth, as well as the immense love and support they are worthy of. I wrote this poem following yet another news story involving the death of a young trans person, and it came from my heart as a gender diverse parent who was thinking about my nonbinary kid, my love for them, and my yearning for a kinder, safer world. As you read, I invite you to reflect on the importance of protecting trans and gender expansive youth, as well as the emotional experiences of gender expansive people like me and my family.

Protection, advocacy, and social change are crucial for the well-being of our trans and gender expansive youth. We must move beyond thoughts and prayers and into advocacy, intentional action, and concrete social change at all levels of government and society. Trans kiddos often face significant threats, bullying, discrimination, and violence, impacting their mental health, physical health, safety, and well-being. For this reason, centering their needs and human rights is a life-saving venture that cannot and should not be delayed. Advocacy is key to creating a world where our kids grow up safely and with the affirming support every child deserves.

Reflective Writing Exercise

Reflect on what it means to feel safe, protected, and supported. Brainstorm ways we can make practical changes that ensure this reality for trans youth. What emotions might you experience in their shoes? How might advocacy impact their sense of self and ability to feel safe in their bodies and the world around them?

Write a poem honoring these explorations. If you feel

comfortable, share this poem in ways that let others know you intend to back up your thoughts with actions.

Sacred Cycles

Final pushes,
baby's borning cry,
midnight meals,
zooming wheels,
nursery rhymes
turned on their head,
and laughter around
the table.

Growing feet,
ball on the street,
pools and splashes,
the first date,
a new license plate,
caps and gowns,
family from out of town.

Wedding day,
birthing your way,
raising them right,
taking flight,
trudging through
the longest night,
last breath,
begin again.

Exhale, Inhale

Exhale binds, constraints
given in little boxes
meant to hamper, slow,
or shrink you.
Exhale all poison
into the sealed void.
Inhale your freedom.

Inhale fresh, clean air,
energy, purpose, truth,
freedom, wide expanses,
fields of wild flowers,
wisdom of ancient trees,
rooted in mushrooming love
and the goodness of your heart.

Transformation Magic

Transformation song
calls to the sun,
rebirth blossoming
from composted pain,
inspiring glitter to rain,
spaciously blanketing
life with the glimmer
of newness and rebirth,
as you dance in creation
of all that is you.

You are Magic

Thought of you today,
radiant heart,
eyes sprinkled with joy.
Through pain, hear me:
Your struggle is not you.
The gift of you still
sparkles through tears.

You are magic, stardust,
safe landing places
for people unseen, unheard.
Let love soak-in now,
envelop you with warmth,
comfort, care, safety, relief.
Your love has multiplied

with every welcome sign
your essence has ever been.
Let it return softly—
nourishment and care.
Let loving kindness
be your comforting tea,
your connection, just be.

More Love, Less Hate

God is love,
and lives in us,
making us love,
original love,
goodness revealed
in healing hands
of a million
cultures, beliefs,
religions, foods,
songs, dances,
breaths.

More of us,
less of hate,
original sin,
songs about
demons within.
Instead, listen
for voices of
Black midwives
Hopi healers,
sacred noadis,
White Tara,
Goddess Aja,
and the child
singing within.

Rescue

Nearly drowned
in oceans of terror,
swallowed in waves,
chariots of confusion.
But love's tide

rushed with purpose
as rescue, relief's electric
energy swallowing noise
with kindness.
Hope's connection brings

gentle healing hands,
resting with care
where body remembers
some sorrow,
but now only knows love.

Hope Remains

When fear chimes
"all is lost,"
remember that time
good news came
just in time,

and a mystery
woman gave
$20 for food,
when last morsels
were already consumed.

Think of meeting
"the one"
after wailing,
lonely in sorrow,
or welcoming a baby
after losing one.

Consider the day after
election day,
when relief brought
assurance of
existence allowed.

Hope is always calling
Fortuna, cornucopia
spinning possibility,
bounties beyond belief.

Laughable Danger

Laugh that danger
right in the face,
stare in its eyes
fearlessly—
all the bigotry,
hatred, discrimination,
gaslighting, rage,
lies, destruction,

see it,

knowing blessed
Omamori manifest
goodness, love,
success, and safety
mighty enough
to piss out the
flames of oppression.

Staying Alive

Staying alive
optimistically,
blooms surround
every part of me
that wonders whether
life will always
be this hard,
sun warming
tear-stained cheeks
with the Eye of Nazar,
swiftly scaring away
every evil force
before it touches me,
granting opportunities
for breath to arrive
at the conclusion
that life is gifting
brave and trusting
soul dances in exchange
for accepting another day.

My Gender

Never fit quite right
until new horizons
opened possibilities
for forging paths
outside binaries,

like finding jeans
that finally button
without squeezing,
or falling down,
the ones that are
soft like jammies,
yet ready for work.

My dreams manifest
comfortably in
these worn-in jeans,
hiding in the back
of my closet, for years
unseen behind

questions wondering
why womanhood was
never quite right,
kind of close,
not really there,
and little kid me
dreamed of being
like grandpa.

Maybe both, neither,
all of the above
spun together the threads

of these work jeans,
ready for board rooms,
bedrooms, hiking trails,
hardware stores,
backyard soil
and so much more
than the 80's
ever dreamed of.

Rest Defiantly

Come to gentle arms
where compassion
envelops hearts
in tender listening,
deep understanding,
warmly needed healing.

When obstacles
10-million stories high
dampen your hopes
for brighter days,
rest defiantly, knowing
grandmothers painted

beautiful futures
with far less,
their wisdom sown
in the soil of your bones,
calling deeply
to show you the way.

Existing Boldly for You

Beyond pain pushing down
lies stunning horizons,
rainbow sunsets,
mountain peaks,

and a small-town grocery
where I almost didn't wear
my Kamala Pride shirt,

missing moments of magic
from a nonbinary kid
running to us with smiles,

freedom, surprise, delight,
beaming from eyes,
the weight of the world
off their shoulders

momentarily
because I removed swords
of fear from mine,

daring to exist boldly,
even, especially here.

Fortune?

No control:
others' bigotry,
racism,
transphobia,
fatphobia,
classism,
genderism,
misogyny,
and on,
and on,
and on,
and intersections of.

Control of:
Noticing sunshine,
listening to birds,
smelling bread bake,
tousling purring fur,
protesting boldly,
accepting help,
watching candle flames
dance as I type,
laughing with children,
enjoying with spouse,
not giving up,
fighting with love,
and hoping subversively,
sometimes uncovering glee.

Staying Put

If people like us
leave country homes,
pushed out by hate,
in favor of city
possibilities,

who will welcome
the next Black,
Queer, Indigenous,
Interracial, Multiracial,
Disabled family
to the neighborhood

with welcome signs
of life in tending tomatoes,
mowing grass, morning walks,
wagging tails, and existing
boldly in the face of it all?

Autumn's Song

Change blankets
this well-worn path
until I lose it,
seeing sameness
in every direction,
inviting release
of all that is known,
blessedly nurturing
grace in loss.

Lotus You

Mud patches settle,
lotus emerging gloriously:
delicately growing,
renewing, blooming
in every morning's rebirth,
following evening's closing:
living and thriving.

Arise, dear lotus:
Bloom past challenges
freely, purposefully now.
Bloom in power,
strength overflowing,
overcoming, overshadowing
until sacred delight remains.

Student of Life

Life marks blackboards
with job loss, cancer,
poverty, bigotry,
and threats to breath,
but also dreams,
hopes refusing death,
even when shattered glass
pummels our hearts,
creating strange lands
inviting ingenuity,
just bold enough
for onlookers to stare,
declaring us plum crazy.

Minnesota Trip

1,407 miles
from our driveway
to my favorite backyard,
hugs, lefse, lingonberries,
Bounce and Tide wafting
from basement laundry
to fresh bowls of raspberries
on the kitchen counter,
next to the Werther's.

Three kids, one dog,
piled with luggage,
even on our laps.
Rest areas in safe places?
Check!
Sundown towns avoided?
Check!
Routes to the best hiking trails,
deep dish, cheese marts, lakes,
and hotel suites for families
printed off?
Check!

Counting down days,
every hour closer
to one more moment
sharing hugs with
the most loving grandparents
and great grandparents
the world has ever known,
grateful we're all still here
to enjoy it.

Blessing for Baby's Voice

May your shining eyes
see more love than fear,
more care than hate,
more inclusion than exclusion,
more peace than war,
more possibilities and goodness
than oppression and terror.

May you always be honored
for the spark of your soul
that warms as you nurse,
for the heart beating simply
for togetherness, love,
and being held in protection.

May your voice always be strong,
and may you never shy away
from voicing needs
like you do so naturally,
so loudly, boldly,
persistently, assuredly
on the first day of life.

PART III: JOY

"And that deep and irreplaceable knowledge of my capacity for joy comes to demand from all of my life that it be lived within the knowledge that such satisfaction is possible."

— AUDRE LORDE, *PARADE*

THOUGHTS ON JOY

MAYA ANGELOU WROTE, "MY MISSION IN LIFE IS NOT merely to survive, but to thrive; and to do so with some passion, some compassion, some humor, and some style.[1]" Joy is fuel for thriving, much like the sunshine that brightens the room when I open the living room curtains early in the morning, just as the sun is beginning to peek over the trees across the street. Its warmth kisses our faces with goodness, whether we are feeling fabulous on a Saturday, about to head to work, or home for a sick day in the middle of the week. No matter the circumstances, that sunshine is a hug directly to our hearts.

Embracing and celebrating joy does not mean there is an absence of pain or complexity; it simply means we give ourselves permission to feast on the goodness of life, even in the midst of challenges, and even when we know that it will not last forever. Good feelings and experiences do not need to last forever to be worthy of celebration or safe to enjoy. When it is accessible to do so, we can set aside our troubles for a little while, and then embrace bounties of delight, enjoyment, love, and goodness as they arrive on our doorstep, using the resources available to us to both relish the world and make it a kinder place.

---

1. *Angelou, Maya. Letter to My Daughter. Random House, 2009, p. 114.*

In doing so, joy sows seeds of generosity and love in ourselves and our communities. It inspires us to wander down new paths and explore fresh, exciting options, causing us to more clearly see what is possible rather than what is impossible. Joy sparks hope. Hope sparks dreams, and dreams build bold new worlds, the kind where the isms that hold us down aren't the systems we're operating under. Those dreams spark courage to act, to spread our wings, and to dare to live with a boldness that inspires positive social change. In the words of Alice Walker, "Resistance is the secret of joy![2]"

---

2. *Walker, Alice. Possessing the Secret of Joy. Simon & Schuster, 1992, p. 288.*

Wonder Becomes Them

Instead of waiting
for wonder to find them
or striving to find it,
they invited it to overtake them
until it became them.

Live Now

Love your dreams, my dear.
Life's timeline refuses pause.
Live now, wondrously.

Ode to Writing

Writing opens spaces,
causes lumps in my throat
when my heart races
as I learn to emote
in words with friends
penning verses and curses,
stories, poems, essays,
as my soul mends,
and trauma disperses
healing grants pathways

to joy with my pen
frolicking with purpose
as I find laughter again
and vow to repurpose
my pain into hopeful
moments of connection
flinging off shame
in favor of soulful
meaningful reflection
as we gather and exclaim

freedom from silence.
We voice narratives
and dance in defiance
calling out imperatives,
sparking wonder,
rebellion in our veins,
writing changes our names,
makes us run with thunder,
throwing off chains,
seeking justice like flames.

Morning Respite

Early morning blankets
plea for unhurried lingering,
as a solitary bird tweets,
welcoming strangers,
revolutionaries, activists,
parading hearts with
gratitude, gladness, celebration.

May delight envelop
every breath, each step,
conscious movement toward
lazy Sunday mornings,
covered in warmth, shelter,
love for all, especially those
new to the safe peace of it.

When Kiddo Paints

Possibilities are infinite
as brushes fashion worlds
into smiling daisies, rainbows,
magical bunnies, gardens,
and whimsical houses
with everyone holding hands.

Love emanates colors,
promises birthing worlds
hopeful with healing, grace,
heartful, gentle,
kind ways of being,

artistic sparks,
readily and boldly
resurrecting goodness.

Canned Tomatoes

Joyfully, tomatoes
take over the house—
one hundred plus
shiny jars
(Grandpa's)
filled with love,
promise, abundance,
dancing, laughter,
clearing for healing,
and maybe salsa,
sauces,
and a kiss
from you,
like that summer
the vines kept giving.

Chosen Family

Friendly eyes,
caring hands,
understanding nods
embolden assured release
of toxic sour fruit,
binds that no longer tie.

In shared presence,
safety frees heart's eyes
to discern intuition boldly,
body and soul guiding,
replacing fear and shame.

In ritual, we celebrate
seasons of change,
unbinding, rebellion,
and boisterous freedom,
letting newness bloom
with ease and grace.

Kamala's Running

Afternoon pool dip,
three kids and me,
celebrating relief
as Kamala centers joy,
and rain pitter patters
on water's surface,
us listening to
underwater rhythm
as we float,
cool blueness
washing away hopelessness
in complete sensory delight.

Healing Hands

Her gentle voice whispers,
"breathe deeply for me,"
as air expands my broad,
queer torso, and embodiment
takes root in care.

Something like relief
unravels my walls,
sprouting wide breaths,
as inner voices invite
yielding to nurture here.

Safe healing hands
rest softly on my ribs,
dissolving trauma within,
as quiet gentle healing
tenderly begins.

Ocean

Carolina blue
ocean possibilities
provide peaceful pause.

Good Morning

Soft morning air
gently awakens peace,
birdsong serenading
every cell joyfully.
Wagging tails proclaim
existence a gift
bathed in goodness.

Lazy mornings kindly
kiss every cell
with simplicity,
nourishing breaths
thankfully,
warming heart's glow—
no place to go,
let's take it slow.

Power of Playfulness

Playfulness waltzes
giddily, creativity healing
through laughter, color,
texture, pattern,
gifts of presence,
connecting hearts,
crafting better worlds.

May delight dance
fairy dust to soaring,
lifted on lightness,
honoring identities
in celebratory chorus,
changing landscapes,
making hate extinct.

Rainbow Blessings

Rainbow-wisdom shines,
painting petals of new blooms,
roots of old growth
connecting heartbeats
with radiant dew,
glittering magic reflected
in morning's first breaths.

Ethereal swirls:
red, orange, yellow,
green, blue, purple,
pink, white, brown, black,
clear paths of wonder,
sunlight bathing skin,
diversity blessing within.

Love's Arrival

Achievements on my wall
are tearful loneliness,
dotted with trauma,
isolation closing in,
as I pray for connection.

Love's arrival drives
four hours in a pickup
with twinkling eyes,
and a smile serenading,
"My, my, my.'

Kisses abundant,
luxurious tingles spreading,
thriving between my thighs,
while nurturing and compassion
connect our hearts wholly.

Holy connection and moans
of pleasurable delight
echo with magical promises,
beautiful and cohesive,
brimming with new life.

Perfect as We Are

Queerness dances delightedly,
as masks of expectation
dissolve magically in flames
of wholehearted authenticity.
Like fire, I am perfect as I am.

Lovingly earthed behind screens,
emerging seen queerness,
precious and vulnerable,
your truth emerges gently.

Breathing, you are perfect as you are.
Bearing souls purposefully,
in mutually cherished reverence,
our eyes lock, twinkle knowingly,
as stories bless the space between us.
A river, we are perfect as we are.

Whispers from My Younger Self

I see rainbow scarves,
knit with care by you.
With supportive embrace,
queer children, too,
and when I do,
I know you're saying
I love you.

I see big bold smiles,
and you breaking free
from religious bonds
saying you can't flee.
Now you can see
how I feel. I'm saying
I love you, too.

Heart's Hope

Belief in hope,
love, joy, delight,
radiates sun beams
delightfully from the heart,
nourishing cells,
our home, our souls,
the dog, the cats,
the kids, and you.

Glowing hearts
begin sweet melodies,
radiating ripples,
renewing earth,
awakening connection,
moving unified goodness,
squashing division.
Rebirth in one breath,
flowing from the heart.

Kindred

Kindred glow,
golden light enveloping
you wholly,
hugging us both,
now glistening rainbows,
illuminating possibilities
just born, now.

First cries—honey,
couriers of courage,
collecting momentum,
changing tides in goodness,
affirmation flying high,
crowds of souls dancing
in movement of love.

See us dance,
hips swaying, arms waving,
grins lighting up,
contagious with laughter.
Joy's power, a change maker,
take-my-hand sayer,
together we go far.

Art Breath

Breathe heartfelt
imperfection, spilling
love like honey,
woven threads
creating rivers,
connecting feltness
in dances of delight.
Human be-ing,
popcorn reading,
heart-led living,
soulful sharing,
empathetic feeling,
compassion multiplying
together, choruses of art.

Healing Breath

Savor this breath,
this one inhale,
lungs expanding,
belly rising, heart full,
appreciation abounding,
doubling and tripling,
until every cell knows love.

Exhale freely now,
appreciation spilling out,
spreading goodness
to waiting souls,
a waiting universe,
ravenous for nourishment
from this one healing breath.

Reflective Pause: Healing Breath

"Healing Breath" reflects on the power of breath for self-care and social change. As part of my daily self-care, I set aside a few intentional minutes to focus on my breathing, becoming aware of my emotional state, my delights, and my needs. I can even use my breath to transform depleting emotions into renewing emotions, or to express care to those I love, like my family or the napping service dog at my feet. While reading, I invite you to consider how simple and intentional breaths might generate positive emotions that make a meaningful difference in your life, not only for your embodied self but also for the world as a whole.

I credit HeartMath for my daily breathwork practice, and I am thankful to them for teaching me how to walk alongside others as they explore the power of their hearts through breath. Several years ago, HeartMath taught me to imagine that my breath was flowing in and out of the area of my heart, allowing it to be gentle, slow, and easy[1]. I can also breathe regenerative feelings like love, appreciation, and care in and out through the area of my heart,[2] then radiate them out to others and the world around me.[3] Doing this helps me to enjoy a sense of overall well-being and increased physiological coherence[4], where my physical, mental, and emotional systems are working together symbiotically, positively impacting those around me.

1. Childre, D., & Martin, H. (1999). *The HeartMath Solution: The Institute of HeartMath's Revolutionary Program for Engaging the Power of the Heart's Intelligence*. HarperOne, p. 92.
2. Childre, D., & Martin, H. (1999). *The HeartMath Solution: The Institute of HeartMath's Revolutionary Program for Engaging the Power of the Heart's Intelligence*. HarperOne, p. 102.
3. Childre, D., & Martin, H. (1999). *The HeartMath Solution: The Institute of HeartMath's Revolutionary Program for Engaging the Power of the Heart's Intelligence*. HarperOne, p. 136.
4. Childre, D., & Martin, H. (1999). *The HeartMath Solution: The Institute of HeartMath's Revolutionary Program for Engaging the Power of the Heart's Intelligence*. HarperOne, p. 64.

Reflective Writing Exercise

Enjoy a few minutes of breathing gently through the area of your heart. Reflect on how this impacts your sense of well-being. Now, think about a stressful situation you encounter regularly, like a meeting at work, interpersonal conflict, or a traffic jam, and imagine breathing this way to find relief. How might your sense of well-being shift?

Write a poem that explores how it feels to center on your breathing during a tense moment, touching on the ripple effects of spreading goodness to others. If you feel comfortable, share this poem with someone who cares about your well-being or who might be interested in trying this practice themselves.

Belonging

Belonging embraces
unsuspecting hearts
with relief and enoughness.
You are welcome here.
You belong.
You are wanted.
We choose you.
Accessibility and welcome,
community opens gently
toward vulnerable risk,
authenticity glowing
in ruby luminescence,
surrounded by mutual souls,
acceptance, inclusion, affirmation,
connection, meaning
deep knowing, tender loving,
patiently trusting that you
(yes you, dear one)
fully, wholly, completely,
entirely, and joyfully fit
here in this fold
where breaths of love
offer hugs of belief.

The Journey

Adieu shoreline,
welcome wild and free,
thriving and delight,
sparkling wonder,
glistening seas,
deep calling spells,
sweet mystical breeze.

Moon invites mystery,
offers rose tea.
Come peer and you'll see:
Way opens, way closes,
sun rises and falls,
tide welcomes and beckons,
a call for us all.

Key West

Joy dances at sunset
for our wedding night.
Ocean roaring,
laughter echoing,
sun dancing portraits,
as we leap for delight,
four bare feet
suspended in leaps,
arms extended,
electric night
as our lives take flight!

Siblings of the Heart

Searching for light,
rainbows burst forth,
heart comets,
offering delight,
beckoning play and

singing: dance with me,
siblings of the heart,
hands joined,
hearts in tune,
our joy is more

than smiles—defiant.
Hate holds no power
next to giddy,
delighted, love-fueled
thriving of the heart.

Service Dog Puppy

Four little paws
poke out first,
before helping
hands arrive.

Her breath
for me, is
her purpose,
to heal
and help.

My inner child
sees beauty
in fluff
licking joy
each day.

Mountain Coasters

Rollercoasters replace hiking
with shouts of delighted joy,
wide thighs rumbling with twists
turns, hills, accelerating
amazement, awe bursting,
fireworks, pores opened,
rising lighthearted giddiness,
roaring laughter echoing,
mountainsides agreeing,
exploding happiness,

heartfully hohoho'ing,
eyes wrinkling, crinkling,
wind whipping through locks,
rainbow shirts blowing freely,
beckoning wisdom from saints,
siblings, friends, scholars,
the woman on the corner,
grandparents whose bones knew
the joy of feeling fully, freely alive!

Heart Focus

Our heart's breath births peace,
radiating love's bright light,
compassion and care.

Christmas Eve 2010

Snowed into our own cozy world
of a bedroom birthing tub.
Christmas Eve, one final push
so the midwife whispers...
Pull your baby out of the water.
Perfect eyes full of wonder.

Heart Knowing

Hearts are made
for running in freedom,
unshackled from expectation,
unencumbered by convention,
laundry lists of shoulds.
Heart's wisdom and breath
shine light, leading soulfully to

unworried soaring, floating,
delighted sparkling through
rainbow spattered,
star speckled skies.
Universe calls in whispers
mystically within you.
Heart knows the way.

Bunches of Goodness

Bunch of dreams,
bunch of love,
bunch of belief,
bunch of shining bright
possibilities, singing everywhere,
all around, with each heartbeat
connecting me to you,
and us to the universe.

Bunch of voices, souls
making goodness brighter,
multiplying purpose, magnifying
the best we could be.
Connection illuminates, now
all things are possible
when we go together.

Sun Drips

Let sun drip to my soul
as unicorns celebrate,
leaping with blooming butterflies,
dreams releasing to fruition,
while wilted beliefs
compost in soil,
feeding something new.

Behold orbs of rainbows,
inspiration blooming intuition,
decisions expressing trust,
authentic soul journeys
thriving in settled mists,
flying on horses: new beginnings,
freedom bounding inward to fly.

Whispers of Healing

Body, whisper songs,
seeds of unknown
mysteries watered,
cooled in healing springs,
wide open spaces,
safely offering care,
ease, freedom, daring

to share gentle roars—
whisper's seed sprouting
like honey from lips.
Waiting ears receive,
caring hearts emote,
healing hands transform
pain to wonder and hope.

Declaration

You are hereby worthy
of extravagant celebration
for boldly trailblazing
past weighted obstacles
surrounding your path.

You thrived daringly,
dancing defiantly,
declaring joy and delight,
leaping on golden tables
that had no chair for you.

Slow Down

Rest in exhales,
cradled in softness,
held by this moment,
quieted by peace
stilled in knowing
all will be well.

It is well on the inhales,
love on the exhales,
as insides slow,
thoughts nap quietly,
as nurture blossoms,
gardens sprout, delight.

Kitten

Candy corn markings,
a purring little nose,
sweet paws,
blue eyes,
and a meow

that brings your face
to life with love,
your baby coloring
childhood with delight,

cuddles, purring,
toys, playing at 2am
when every parent and
sibling is fast asleep.

Kitchen Kid

One cat apron,
whisk, spatula,
glass dishes of spices, and
a bowl of gluten-free flour.

Four eggs,
some fruit,
one glowing, radiant child,
whisking love into magic,
ready to be consumed.

Scents of cinnamon,
nutmeg, ginger,
and laughter,
little hands stirring dreams,
the music of her heart.

Bodacious Body Love

Bodacious body,
round and soft,
gentle curves winding,
flowers blooming,
tender, pleasing,
delightfully sensuous,
worthy of care,
protection, celebration.

Let delight embrace,
warmly cradle,
tantalize every
blessed dip and valley,
each inch with love
so bold, extravagant,
goodness is the singular
song ears now hear.

Mountain Day

Mountains of my heart,
you cradle us warmly
in outstretched branches,
paths of goodness,
exhaling stress as
your breath expands,
happiness overflowing,

no matter what bank balance,
world events, challenges,
delights and celebrations
have visited our lives,
twisting emotions into
paintings of realness.

You welcome us with
words of whisper in
winds of wisdom,
wanting wonderful
wishes, dreams of
togetherness to blossom,
saying we belong.

Pride Rhythm

See Black Pride,
rhythms of celebration
this one for you,
blessed perfection,
beauty in every part of you.

Every gender, age,
shape, preference,
everyone strutting paths,
waving hips, clapping hands,
feet tapping, lips whistling,

affirming, boldly lighting,
purposeful, daring souls,
unafraid to resist joyfully,
success and happiness raining
rainbows everywhere.

Very Gender

They are themself,
embracing goodness
soaring as comets
outside parameters,
beyond stars seen,
thriving spectacularly,

brightness illuminating
bits of eyeliner,
mixed with partially
shaved heads,
sprinkled with punk,
confidence blossoming
magnificently.

They are important,
their life's breath
sparkling everywhere
their soul and feet
waltzing with trails
of yellow, white,
purple, and black.

See how they
transform worlds
with radical kindness,
welcoming all,
understanding and
support setting
new world records,

thriving daringly,
paving new roads

for kids without maps,
daring to reach out
hands to the friendless.

Nonbinary kid,
affirming worthy persons,
loved with every breath.

Affirming Spaces

Melodies dance magic,
spawn tempos uniting
heartbeats—one rhythm,
inclusion weaving
vapors of rainbows,
glowing great goodness.

Affirming breaths
delight children dancing,
twirling in light,
dotted and speckled,
sparkling and glowing,
celebrated, love lauded.
Tears of joy: Relief—
hope fertilized today.

Inner Trust

Trust yourself,
your internal knowing
faithfully guides ahead,
opening new doors,
sprouting self-assurance,
queerly quieting noise,
granting peaceful purpose

with magic wands,
glittering possibilities
blanketing like pollen,
sans the sneeze,
plus fuels of delight,
dancing in the sparkles,
soaring in lifted radiance.

The Gift

Restless energy
creates journeys
birthing in wonder,
mapping alignment,
yesses swinging
wildly with laughter,
inspiring new cycles,
divine harmony
authentically
expressing trust,
knowing Panacea
blooms elixirs
within my dreams,
sharing healing,
calm peace
from my heart
to yours.

Young Peace

Dove settles my heart,
finally flying in,
soaring freely, easily
on compassion's wings.
With tenderness, warmth
cozies up, hope arising,
meeting needs gently.
Younger selves smile
within, finally welcomed,
heard, embraced gratefully,
listening ears ready,
as stories and wisdom
light flowered paths—
purpose, delight, joy.
We journey together.

Kid Comes Out

Coming out,
stars guide you,
witnessing joy,
bravery blossoming
in this pot of gold,
wishes incarnate,
rainbows end
made flesh
among us, boldly
manifesting riches
of peace, protection,
kindness, sunshine
of highest good,
desires supporting
unconditional soulfulness,
wildly celebrating love.

Community-Care

Hold me here
as I hold you,
splashing, delighting
in goodness and
the relief of
letting go
of being alone.

Joy sees
others emerge warmly,
fog clearing,
uncovering crowds
of love waiting,
arms outstretched,
antsy, anticipating
worldwide embrace.

Uncontained

Here I am,
truth bursting proudly,
truly uncontained,
throwing off everything
ill-fitting and not me,
especially masks,
revealing my face
wholeheartedly,
new eyes seeing
the beauty of you,
soul bared, mask
discarded.
Vulnerably, we dance.

Thriving

This clearing,
wide and spacious,
chances fruition,
finally free,
frolicking future
plans giving growth,
subverting convention,
joyful labor
setting roots,
growing shoots,
muddying boots,
boldly balancing
blessings ordained,
diamonds of Armid
watering earth,
herbs inducting
magic.

Gifts

This vining plant,
my kid's cutting,
has given birth
twenty times over

like the lines of this
notebook multiply
the words from
my heart

and the glowing
candle offers
a wellspring of ideas
never running dry.

Boldly You

Be your voice,
not silent, but assured,
unshakable presence,
courageously authentic,
unwaveringly unmoved,
thriving with momentum,
love's unstoppable force.

Be present,
claim your belonging.
Young youth watch,
walk as you walk,
glow in self-worth,
rainbows of identities,
humanity overflowing
because you are you.

Remember Your Care

Remember yourself
in caring for others.
Remember your dreams
as your seeds sprout
within your neighbor's garden.
Sow in your soil, too.
Fertilize there, too.

Tend your own garden
until love's seed matures,
blowing in the wind,
burrowing in land
of every neighbor,
and their neighbor.
Sprout love everywhere.

Life Now

Free schedules,
candlelight,
donated food,
and little money,
yet community

(intersectional)

connects worlds
gratefully,
passionate poems
killing imprisoned
dispassion
with nourishment.

Reflective Pause: Abundance

"Life Now" was written to capture the abundance of connection and love during a trying financial situation. At the end of 2022, I was laid off from a 14-year writing contract, and in February 2023, my spouse was laid off from a nearly 24-year engineering position, leaving us without meaningful income. To add insult to injury, I contracted long COVID, and he was diagnosed with cancer, underwent surgery, and survived complications.

Yet, despite it all, there was great abundance of other kinds. We found ourselves enjoying each other's company, savoring the goodness of little things, feeling overwhelmingly grateful for having our needs met, and surrounded by a worldwide community that offers generous support, help, and love. Indeed, our circumstances created space for me to write poems like the ones in this collection, and for both my spouse and me to enjoy doing the things that feed our souls in ways that might fully support our family financially into the future.

Reflective Writing Exercise

Reflect on a time when you felt a deep sense of gratitude for the non-material abundance in your life, such as the support of friends, the beauty of nature, the generosity of others, or the joy of creative expression. How do these things help you navigate the challenges of life?

Write a poem sharing non-material gratitude, exploring what brings you joy and purpose. If you feel comfortable, share your poem with those in your community who make a difference in your life.

Election Hopes

New journeys
explore promises fulfilled,
rejoicing in streets,
running with goodness,
desire aligning purpose,
as hope sees possibility
once boarded,
now freed,
Maneki Neko
purring in delight,
pink and green
waves rising,
relief offering
miraculous birthing
of endless soirees.

Believe in You

I believe in you.
If only you knew
how the world waits
for words only you
hold tenderly, warmly
in your heart.
Release them.

See your voice move
light: hearts waiting.
Words comfort
as striving sleeps,
so bright blooms
open with wonder,
gifts beyond belief.

Caring Freely

Because I can,
bright orange
nail polish
dots my toes
with sparkles,

chai rooibos
tickles my nose,
as heart breaths
slow my worries
until they pivot,

remembering that
caring freely
for myself
is revolutionary
in worlds

not built for my
thriving,
so now I am
ready for
the fight.

(Thank you, Audre Lorde.)

Affirming Care

After the last therapist,
your warm welcome
opens safe spaces
for my true self
to gaze inward
admiringly,
believing I am worthy
of love.

Affirming complexities
of intersectional living,
my pain is recognized
as human, as valid,
as trauma in need
of healing,
rather than
merely "political."

Here, I am enough,
worthy of kindness,
generosity, care,
rest, love,
connection,
goodness and beauty,
simply because

I have breath in my lungs,
a beat in my heart,
and longings from a soul
beginning to heal.

Home

Home is here with you,
Hospital rooms or bedrooms,
Hearts radiate love

Pansexual Marriage

means I love you
and would have
loved you,
no matter what
gender, identity,
expression,
or body change
presented itself
over all these
decades,
because I love
the essence
of stardust
embedded in
your sparkling soul,
the wisdom, beauty,
breathtakingly
stunning glory
of your beating heart.
I love you
for you.

Heart Wisdom

Engulfing heart,
life's lantern loving
worlds of possibilities,
whispers wisdoms,
waiting, wanting,
to cozy up with
each and every cell,
advising spaces
of rest and renewal,
connecting humanity
in one sacred drum.

Home's Embrace

Welcome home,
settle into softness,
relief longed for,
dear weary traveler.
Cushions sweetly envelop
aching, throbbing places,
cozying heart to soul.

Heart wisdom blooms
in tender hands, quiet
listening moments,
love's waves calming
minds like still waters,
thoughts like canoes,
glide by with peace.

Rainbows of Delight

Rivers of rainbows,
prisms dance, affirm,
celebrate magnificently
gleaming, shining cells,
stunning tip to toe,
held and sublime,
now is your time.

Belonging beckons
brightly beaming
brushstrokes of beauty
becoming bountiful,
boisterous, ballets,
dances of diversity
daring to delight tonight.

Words

Breathe words
to change, heal,
transform the world,
embrace the world,
un-other the world
of margins,
crumbling walls
of echo chambers

until the softest
voices are loudest,
centered, treasured,
amplified, multiplied,
heard with words
replenishing cauldrons
of the magic
we were meant to be.

Kitchen Magic

Your heart
creates spells
of love
on cutting boards,
or bubbling soups,
through spices,
reminding deepest
desires that wishes
do come true,
nourished in
supportive hands,
intuition welcoming
changes mirroring
growing energy,
bravery brewing big.

Slow Magic

Rosemary-mint
wafting on notes
of apple tea,
dancing like fire
in this orchard candle,
as incense invites
ingenuity, creativity
weaving magic,
birds chirping joy
through window screens,
inviting cool breezes
to caress my heart's
creative stirrings,
appreciating nuances
of soul progress,
exciting embrace
of challenging
new horizons.

Mountain Fall

Fog's silent whisper,
yellow leaves drift downward now,
fall blessing mountains.

Graduation Day

Pregnant with you
one hot May day,
belly barely zipped
into a big black gown,
we shake hands
with every brilliant Black
theological scholar responsible
for generously sharing wisdom,

imparting skills to
question everything,
feasting vibrantly,
sumptuously savoring
this loving soul journey,
rainbow wisdom sprouting,
beginning to take root,
birthing our new way of life.

Dance

If magic resides
within your cells
(it does),
let it dance:
freestyle, tap,
jazz, hip hop,
ballet, waltz.

Let magic dance
wildly, no restraints,
no limits imposed
on who, what,
when, where, why,
how you shine,
dancing with strangers.

Simplicity

I need nothing
more than this view—
waves crashing,
gulls singing,
holding hands
in the sand
with you.

Yes

Yes, my heart,
to new horizons,
dreams imagined,
longingly long ago,
with warmth,
excitement, joy
uncontainable.
Yes to you.

Yes to younger you,
hoping for someone
ready to play,
to silence
old voices
with singing
today, oh
to them I say:
Delight in it!

This Magical Door

opens to
rainbow paradises,
overflowing richness,
inclusion bursting
with delight.

The nonbinary
friend in a
decked out
wheelchair,
painted to match
their rainbow
dreadlocks,
cranks the tunes,
feet tapping,
uproarious laughter.

Neon signs signal
the most marginalized lives
embrace, boldly claim
empowerment, centering,
and inclusion here.
Enchanting community,
intentionally accessible
for anyone
who dares
open the door.

Gathering Life

as my arms
gather goodness
from above me
with every inhale,
tippy toes extending,
reaching for more
than I can ever carry,
floor boards creaking,
furry one panting,
morning sun filtering
through closed curtains,
the air carrying
ravenous hunger for
delights, joys, pleasures,
even as creaking knees
remind me every day
is as much a gift
as this one gentle step.

Chocolate Cake

My honey measures
gluten-free flour,
sugar, eggs,
fair-trade
cocoa powder,
vanilla extract,
and heaping portions
of love
every year
on my birthday.

Two layers,
rich fudge frosting,
my contribution,
because he tried once,
resulting in
a gooey
chocolatey mishap.
(I'm glad to help.)

Juicy fresh raspberries,
my favorite, and
an extra kiss
of his sweet love
pile on top
before he sings,
three kids in chorus,

as I remember
Gramme's love
for the same
luxurious decadence,

savoring an
extra slice,
just for her.

Refuge

Today, my office door
closed gently behind,
keeping the music
of silence for myself.

Diffuser hums
to the tune of
crackling candle
flames waltzing,

undisturbed breaths
deepening, delightfully
calming racing
thoughts

with appreciation
for simple joys
in hot tea,
handmade chocolate
melting.

Dreaming

With my eyes open,
I watch you step tentatively
into vibrant community, affirmed,
celebrating identity, laughter,
courage and faith.

Twirling melanin and magic,
joyfully dancing, healing hearts
with elixirs of life,
oceans of time release stress
as nourishment abounds.

Witchy Friends

Fat and fabulous,
dancing and dreaming,
crying and caring,
sharing and daring,
music playing,
feet tapping,
rhythm creating
love from heartbeats,
shared hope,
intentions,
not tensions,
moving worlds
freshly toward
loving, expressive
soul influences
of highest good,
listening in
authentic, creative
empowerment,
catapulted in
synergy on this
fucking fabulous
life journey.

Reflective Pause: Community

"Witchy Friends" celebrates the vibrant, empowering, and transformative energy of friendship and community. It is based on my experience in being part of a mostly fat, mostly queer witch circle that meets via Zoom several times a year. We gather to offer support, encouragement, and set intentions on holidays that correspond with the seasons. This is a safe space where everyone is welcomed, included, and affirmed exactly as they are.

As you read this poem, I invite you to reflect on the power of authentic connection and the joy of shared experiences. Consider how safe relationships create spaces that spark synergy, empowerment, energy, empathy, encouragement, and joy, fueling us to thrive as we navigate our life journeys. In moments of dancing, dreaming, crying, and caring, we find ourselves surrounded by friends who share our hopes and desires. Together, we create better worlds with loving and expressive intentions for our highest good.

Reflective Writing Exercise

Reflect on a time when you felt deeply connected to your friends or community, in ways that made it feel safe to fully be your authentic and vulnerable self. Focus on the sense of empowerment, joy, and freedom that resulted. How did these connections influence your life journey and personal growth?

Write a poem exploring these experiences, considering how important relationships help you navigate life's ups and downs. If you feel comfortable, share your poem with your community, honoring the love that you share together.

Blessing for Protection

May energies of protection
guide gently onward,
clearing flowered paths,
blessing soulful dreams,
igniting spoken plans
with sparks of joy,
assurance, jeweled hands.

May eyes of truth
delight love's purpose,
melodically singing hearts,
heartfully open minds,
swirling soulful confidence,
blooming in mysterious,
ethereal fogs of goodness.

AFTERWORD

I am overwhelmingly grateful for the gift of spending time with you through this book. The writing shared here has emerged from deeply personal processing of some of the life experiences my family has endured and celebrated through being queer and interracial in the rural South. I hope some of the poems have resonated with you in ways that make you feel less alone, or that they have given you a window into another's lived experience in ways that make you want to make the world a kinder place.

In other areas of my professional life, I am honored to serve as the founding executive director of a nonprofit dedicated to offering healing services to people who have experienced human trafficking, as well as their family members. In both my nonprofit work and my private practice, I am a certified Othmer Method neurofeedback practitioner, HeartMath Interventions and Resilient Heart provider, trauma-sensitive coach, human trafficking consultant, and writing coach. Walking alongside people as they navigate their healing journeys, process their life experiences, and build lives of thriving brings great joy and purpose to my life.

The tools I incorporate into my everyday life and work with clients are designed to nurture our well-being, especially in the context of living with intersectionality and being people with hearts to seek social change. Practices such as intentional breathing, qigong, writing, art, and spending time in nature help us take time to refuel and care for ourselves in essential ways. As Tricia Hersey says, "You were not just born to center your entire existence on work and labor. You were born to heal, to grow, to be of service to yourself and community, to practice, to experiment, to create, to have space, to dream, and to connect."[1]

To connect with more of my writing or inquire about support offerings, please visit my website (www.annekinsey.com) and follow me on Instagram at @anne.kinsey.writes. It would be my heart's great delight to continue to encourage and relate with you in meaningful ways.

I am grateful to Tehom Center Publishing for their commitment to elevating marginalized voices. Their support has been invaluable in bringing this book to life. If you are writing from the margins and hope to find a publisher that values amplifying your unique voice, I encourage you to contact them at www.tehomcen ter.org .

Thank you once again for joining me on this journey. May we continue to connect, heal, inspire, and create change.

With Gratitude,
Anne Kinsey

1. Hersey, Tricia. *Rest Is Resistance: A Manifesto*. Little, Brown Spark, 2022, p. 13.

Acknowledgments

First and foremost, I want to express my deepest gratitude to my spouse, Allen, for walking by my side, enjoying the adventure of life with me, supporting my work and believing in my dreams. Your deep love has been my anchor. To my kids, Will, River, and Becca, thank you for inspiring me, loving me, and cheering me on. You are my greatest joy and motivation.

To my friends, too numerous to list, including the BPM cohort, your support has been invaluable. Malumir, thank you for being someone who gets it, who connects in meaningful ways, and shares the writing life with me. Your companionship has made this journey more enjoyable. Kathy, you have been there for me since we were little kids, and you continue to inspire me with how you chase your dreams. Thank you for your enduring friendship.

Patricia and my witch circle friends, thank you for providing safe spaces to tend to my heart. Your support has been a source of strength. Asher and my fat community friends, thank you for being an affirming home base. Your acceptance, affirmation, and love have been a refuge. Trish, our conversations as your magical hands keep me mobile have left me with a greater sense of well-being and belief in myself. Thank you for your care and support. Diana, your publishing connections opened doors to affirming spaces that I am forever grateful for, and our monthly meetings are fuel for my writer's heart. I treasure your friendship.

Beth Kempton, thank you for your mentoring and guidance. Your wisdom has been a guiding light. Theresa and Linda, thank you for encouraging me to pursue my own path so many years ago at Hamline University. Your belief in me set the foundation for my journey. Cai, thank you for opening a safe, affirming space for me to process, heal, and grow. To my professors and friends from ITC and Hood Seminary, thank you for shaping the questions I ask and changing the ways I engage with the world. Your influence so many years ago changed the course of my life.

Thank you, also, to the other friends, mentors, acquaintances, and strangers who have supported and encouraged me and my work. There are too many of you to name, yet I would not be who I am today without you.

Finally, to Tehom Center Publishing, the TCP Facebook group, and Angela Yarber, thank you for saying yes to my dream and walking by my side to bring it to fruition. Your support has made this book possible.

www.ingramcontent.com/pod-product-compliance
Lightning Source LLC
Jackson TN
JSHW060037050325
80000JS00005B/11

* 9 7 8 1 9 6 6 6 5 5 0 8 4 *